$24.67

D0500625

The Triangle Shirtwaist
Factory Fire

Events That Shaped America

Sabrina Crewe and Adam R. Schaefer

Gareth Stevens Publishing

A WORLD ALMANAC EDUCATION GROUP COMPANY

Please visit our web site at: www.garethstevens.com
For a free color catalog describing Gareth Stevens Publishing's list of high-quality
books and multimedia programs, call 1-800-542-2595 (USA) or 1-800-387-3178
(Canada). Gareth Stevens Publishing's fax: (414) 332-3567.

Library of Congress Cataloging-in-Publication Data available upon request from publisher.
Fax (414) 336-0157 for the attention of the Publishing Records Department.

ISBN 0-8368-3402-X

This North American edition first published in 2004 by
Gareth Stevens Publishing
A World Almanac Education Group Company
330 West Olive Street, Suite 100
Milwaukee, WI 53212 USA

This edition © 2004 by Gareth Stevens Publishing.

Produced by Discovery Books
Editor: Sabrina Crewe
Designer and page production: Sabine Beaupré
Photo researcher: Sabrina Crewe
Maps and diagrams: Stefan Chabluk
Gareth Stevens editorial direction: Jim Mezzanotte
Gareth Stevens art direction: Tammy Gruenewald

Photo credits: Corbis: pp. 9, 12, 14, 19; The Granger Collection: pp. 5, 26; Kheel Center,
Cornell University: cover, pp. 4, 11, 16, 17, 18, 21, 22, 23, 24, 25; Library of Congress:
p. 7; North Wind Picture Archives: pp. 6, 8, 13, 20; UNITE: p. 27.

Printed in the United States of America

1 2 3 4 5 6 7 8 9 08 07 06 05 04

Contents

Introduction

The Triangle Factory

The Triangle factory was a clothes-making shop in New York City. Hundreds of women and a few men went to work there every day, crowded into the top three floors of the ten-story Asch building in downtown Manhattan. There, the workers cut and sewed shirtwaists, a type of women's blouse popular in the early 1900s. Most of the workers were young women and girls, recent **immigrants** from Europe, between the ages of thirteen and twenty-three.

Trapped by Fire

On the afternoon of March 25, 1911, a fire broke out on the eighth floor of the Asch building. At the time, there were about five hundred people in the factory. Most escaped, but many were trapped by the fire. Firefighters did everything they could, but they could not reach those who were trapped high up. In the end, 146 people burned to death or died jumping from the building to get away from the flames.

Time for Change

Why were the workers trapped? The Triangle factory owners knew their factory was dangerous, but they did nothing to protect their employees. In the early 1900s, millions of men, women, and children went to work in dangerous places. There were no laws to make sure that places of work were safe and clean. The poor were so desperate for work that they spent their days in horrible conditions, working long hours for little money. For many, it was a terrible situation, but it took a tragic fire to make the wealthier citizens in American society realize that **reforms** were needed in the workplace.

Stained with Blood

"The floods of water from the firemen's hose that ran into the gutter were actually stained red with blood. I looked upon the heap of dead bodies and I remembered these girls were the shirtwaist makers. I remembered their great strike of last year in which these girls had demanded more **sanitary** conditions and more safety precautions in the shops. These dead bodies were the answer."

William G. Shepherd, Triangle fire eyewitness and United Press reporter, March 27, 1911

Women and children process vegetables in a crowded canning factory. In the early 1900s, people had no rights to decent working conditions or pay.

Chapter One

The Move to the Cities

Big Changes in the 1800s

In the early days of the United States, most people were farmers. Before the mid-1800s, there were few factories, and people made or grew many of the things they needed.

Then the country began to change. In the middle and late 1800s, many new inventions were created. With the coming of **industry** and machines, people didn't need to make everything themselves, and large manufacturing companies started to appear. This period of change is known as the Industrial Revolution, when all kinds of developments happened at the same time.

During the Industrial Revolution, huge steelworks such as this one sprang up in and around U.S. cities. They changed a landscape of fields and farms into one of smoky factories.

Mulberry Street in New York City, with its busy market, was a center for many immigrants from Europe.

New Demands

The coming of railroads opened up new opportunities—now people and goods could move around the country much more easily. This led to other new demands: for building materials, for fuel such as coal and oil, for new machines, and for packaged and processed foods. New farming tools meant people did not need to spend all their time growing food anymore. Many workers left farms and went to work in factories making machines, tools, trains, and all the other new things that were changing their lives.

The Need for Workers

More and more factories sprang up in cities, and a huge labor force was needed to work in them. But it took more than just American farm workers to fill the factories. Between 1865 and 1873, about three million immigrants came to the United States from Europe, hoping for good jobs and the chance to escape from overcrowded European cities. American cities grew fast and got just as crowded as the places people had left behind in Europe.

Rapid Changes
"There is nothing in all the past to compare with the rapid changes now going on in the civilized world. . . . The snail's pace . . . has suddenly become the headlong rush of the locomotive, speeding faster and faster."

Henry George, Social Problems, *1883*

Most newcomers to the city lived in multistory **tenement** houses. These were hastily constructed by landlords and builders eager to make money, and they weren't very well built. Tenement buildings were also dark and dirty, and many poor immigrant families of ten or fifteen people lived in one room. The best tenement houses had two toilets on each floor, while some had just one in a courtyard at the bottom of the building. By the late 1800s, large American cities were terrible places to live, at least for the poor. Sickness and starvation raged through the tenements. Nobody could afford doctors or medicine, and many thousands of people died as a result.

A New York tenement in the 1800s.

The Factories

European immigrants found themselves working in awful conditions. Factories generally had bad **ventilation** and no heating. They were overcrowded with people, equipment, and materials, and fires and accidents could easily occur. People were frequently injured and even killed by the machines they operated. **Unsanitary** conditions caused workers to get sick, but they could not afford to stay home, and so illness would spread throughout the factories.

The Rules of Work

In these horrible conditions, people were required to work as many hours and days as their employers demanded, or they would lose their jobs. They were often forbidden to take breaks, even to use the toilet or eat a meal. It was not just adults who had to labor in these awful circumstances. Children also had to work if their families were to scrape by. From as young as six years old, they toiled alongside adults in factories and were expected to work just as long and hard.

Utter Wretchedness and Misery

"... half a million men, women and children are living in the tenement houses of New York. . . . No brush could paint or pencil describe . . . the utter wretchedness and misery, the vice and crime, that may be found within a stone's throw of City Hall, even within an arm's length of many churches. . . . From the nearly 200,000 tenement houses come 93 percent of the deaths and 90 percent of the crimes of our population."

Harper's Weekly *magazine, 1876*

Children were used as cheap labor by factory owners in the late 1800s and early 1900s. These children are working the spinning machines in a textile factory.

Chapter Two

Fighting for Change

The Growth of Unions

American workers knew that factory-owners were getting rich from their hard labor. But there was not much a single worker could do to make owners improve working conditions. By the late 1800s, however, many workers were joining **unions**, which fought for changes in the workplace. As the workforce grew, so did the size and power of the unions.

To make factory owners listen to their protests, unions could call workers out on **strike**. This was when employees stopped work until employers agreed to their demands.

In the early 1900s, **suffragettes** campaigned for women's rights. These women are marching in a 1911 parade.

Working Women

In the 1800s, women were not considered equal to men. They couldn't vote, and at first they were not allowed to join unions. But by 1895, there were 5 million women working in the United States, and they began to form their own unions. By the early 1900s, more than half of all union members in the garment industry were women. The International Ladies' Garment Workers' Union (ILGWU), founded in 1900, helped female clothes makers. The Women's Trade Union League (WTUL) was formed in 1903. It was a combination of poor workers and wealthy **reformers**.

Shirtwaist Workers Go on Strike

In 1909, more than thirty thousand people, most of them women, worked in New York City's five hundred shirtwaist factories. They were becoming increasingly angry at their working conditions.

On November 9, 1909, five hundred workers at the Triangle Shirtwaist Company went on strike to protest their working conditions. Two weeks later, they were joined by about twenty thousand **garment** workers from several hundred other factories. Known as the "Uprising of the Twenty Thousand," this strike was the first large-scale strike of female workers in the United States.

Tired of Listening
"I am a working girl, one of those on strike against intolerable conditions. I am tired of listening to speakers who talk in general terms. What we are here for is to decide whether we shall or shall not strike. I offer a resolution that a general strike be declared now!"

Clara Lemlich, garment worker and union activist, November 22, 1909

Women filled the Cooper Union hall in New York City on November 22, 1909. They voted for a general strike of shirtwaist makers to support the workers already on strike.

11

Strikers stand outside their workplace during the shirtwaist strike in February 1910. They were on strike for several months and received no pay from their employers.

What They Wanted

The strikers wanted better pay and shorter working days. They also wanted to be allowed to join unions so that they could be represented in the workplace. And they wanted their employers to improve their factories. In particular, they wanted the factories made safer from fire.

On the Picket Line

Shirtwaist workers **picketed** all day outside their places of work. They marched and carried signs demanding owners improve the factories. The women got very cold, and they were attacked and beaten by men hired by the factory owners. The police arrested them, even though what they were doing was perfectly legal. Many strikers were fined or sent to jail.

At first, the factory owners refused to listen to the workers' demands, and the strike continued into 1910. It was very hard on the families of striking workers.

The Strike Comes to an End

Eventually, most companies gave in and agreed to a shorter workweek and higher wages. The shirtwaist strike officially ended on February 15, 1910. The Triangle factory's owners, however, never gave in. The Triangle employees went back to work when the other shirtwaist workers did, but nothing had changed. They still worked fifty-nine hours a week for the same pay as before, and the Asch building where the factory was housed had not been made any safer.

This room full of garment workers is like the workrooms in the Triangle factory, where the fire broke out in 1911.

The Triangle factory was on the top three floors of the Asch building. The fire broke out on the eighth floor.

The Asch Building

The Triangle workers had good reason to ask for an improvement in fire safety. Four fires had occurred at their building in the ten years before the strike, but nothing had been done to improve conditions.

The Asch building was ten stories high and was supposed to have three staircases, but it only had two. This fact had been ignored by New York City's Building Department and Fire Department when their officials approved the building for use.

The building had no sprinkler system, and the fire escape only went down to the second floor, 20 feet (6 meters) above the ground. Worst of all, the doors that led to the stairs from the Triangle workrooms were locked from the outside during working hours so the employees could not steal anything and sneak off. The women had asked their employers to stop locking them in, but the factory owners continued to do so.

Inspections

In 1909, a fire prevention expert inspected the Triangle factory. He said the factory should have fire drills. He also said the company should stop locking employees in and should do something about overcrowding on its three floors.

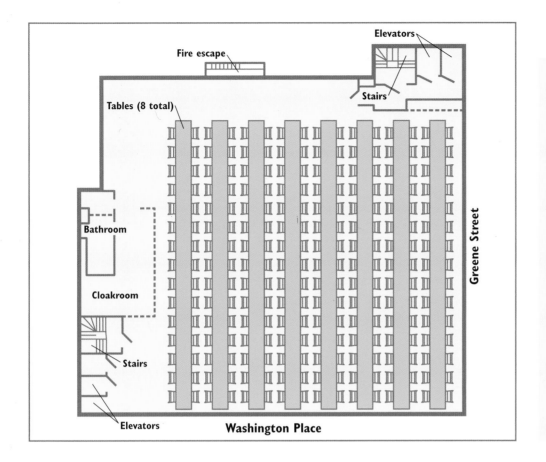

A floor plan of the Triangle factory shows how 240 sewing stations were squeezed around eight long tables on the ninth floor.

The Triangle factory owners ignored all these suggestions. In spite of its potential dangers, the Asch building passed a routine fire inspection in October 1910, just a few months before the fire broke out.

A Warning Ignored

On November 25, 1910, a factory in Newark, New Jersey, caught fire. Workers were trapped in the building, and twenty-five people died. New York City Fire Chief Edward Croker warned that the same sort of thing could happen in his city. He told local newspapers, "A fire in the daytime would be accompanied by terrible loss of life."

One person who read Croker's words was a professor at New York University, and he immediately wrote a letter to the New York City Building Department. He said that he could see crowded and unsafe conditions in the Asch building across the street from his classroom window. The city did nothing about his warning.

Chapter Three

Fire

This cutting room in the early 1900s has rolls of fabrics stacked up (left) and a floor littered with fabric scraps. In the Triangle factory, the scraps and rolls that were piled up high helped the fire to spread rapidly.

Fire on the Eighth Floor

In the late afternoon of March 25, 1911, most workers in the Asch building had gone home, but there were still close to five hundred Triangle workers in the factory.

Nobody is sure how the fire actually started, but it began on the eighth floor and spread very quickly. The workers and supervisors threw several pails of water on the flames, but the fire continued to grow.

Some workers got out through the door and down the stairs on the Greene Street side before the stairs caught fire. The remaining eighth-floor workers began to panic. They jammed up against the door on the Washington Place side of the cutting room, making it impossible to open. Several groups managed to get down using the elevators, and some workers crawled out of the windows and onto the fire escape. They slipped and fell down to the

This cutting room in the early 1900s has rolls of fabrics stacked up (left) and a floor littered with fabric scraps. In the Triangle factory, the scraps and rolls that were piled up high helped the fire to spread rapidly.

sixth floor, where one worker broke a sixth-floor window and they all climbed back inside. They were then trapped by locked interior doors, but fortunately the fire had not yet spread to the sixth floor.

THE LOCKED DOOR!

An illustration published after the fire shows an artist's image of the workers locked inside a workroom as flames engulf them.

On the Tenth Floor

As the fire reached the tenth floor, frantic workers headed to the elevators and stairways. Soon, however, all paths leading down to safety were cut off by fire, and people began to push their way through the smoke up to the roof. Among these people were the owners of the Triangle factory, Isaac Harris and Max Blanck, along with two of Blanck's young children.

The people on the tenth floor were lucky because they could reach the roof. Almost seventy people were on the tenth floor, but only one died—a young woman who jumped from a window before anyone could stop her.

A Living Picture

"There was a living picture in each window—four screaming heads of girls waving their arms. 'Call the firemen,' they screamed—scores of them. 'Get a ladder,' cried others. . . . We cried to them not to jump."

William G. Shepherd, eyewitness and United Press reporter, March 27, 1911

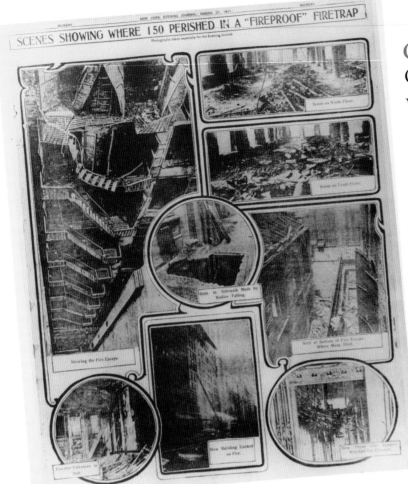

These newspaper photographs show the collapsed fire escape; the burned wreckage of the ninth and tenth floors; and a crumpled elevator.

On the Ninth Floor

On the ninth floor, the workers had gathered their coats from the cloakroom when they saw flames breaking in the windows. They started screaming and running to the doors, but the managers had locked the door to the Washington Place stairs, and the Greene Street stairwell was already in flames.

In the smoke and confusion, many groups of workers were pushing against each other, trying to find a way out. The high shaft that contained the elevators was open, and several workers at the front of the crowd were shoved into the gaping hole. They plunged to their deaths, and their bodies jammed the elevators at the bottom.

Falling Bodies

"We came tearing down Washington Square East and made the turn into Washington Place. The first thing I saw was a man's body come crashing down through the sidewalk shed of the school building. We kept going. We turned into Greene Street and began to stretch in our hoses. The bodies were hitting around us."

Frank Rubino, New York City firefighter

One of the girls in the workroom was able to break a window, and dozens rushed out onto the fire escape. Some ran down the escape and re-entered the building on the sixth floor. But then the rickety fire escape—unable to handle the weight of so many people—collapsed, hurling the workers into the street below.

Help Arrives

The elevators were jammed, fire had cut off the stairways, and the fire escape had collapsed. But there was some help on the way. A policeman ran into the building and let out the women trapped behind the locked doors on the sixth floor. Firefighters arrived on the scene six minutes after the fire started and immediately stormed into the building. They battled the flames in the stairwell as they tried to work their way up to the people trapped at the top.

Students from the university building opposite managed to rescue some people from the tenth floor. They ran ladders across from their roof to the Asch building roof and helped the workers walk across to safety.

When the firefighters arrived, they found their ladders would not reach the top of the building. They aimed their hoses high to try and dampen the flames on the upper floors.

Leaping out of buildings onto safety nets was sometimes the only way to escape a fire, as shown in this picture from the 1890s. The Triangle workers jumped bravely, but the nets failed to save them.

Trapped

Many people were still trapped inside. For them, there was only one way out—to jump. Down on the street, firefighters held out brand new safety nets for the women to land on. But the nets broke, and the women crashed through to the sidewalk. The firefighters tried reaching the women with a ladder, but it only went up to the sixth floor.

When the trapped workers could not bear it any longer, they began jumping from the ledge of the ninth floor, even though they knew they would die. The crowds watching below wailed and sobbed as one worker after another fell to her death.

When the firefighters finally reached the ninth floor, they put out the fire in only a half hour. But it was too late. Sixty-two people had died jumping from the burning building.

At the morgue, people filed by the coffins looking for missing relatives. Seven bodies were still unclaimed six days after the fire.

The Victims

In the end, 146 people lost their lives in the Triangle fire. The police found thirty-six bodies in an elevator shaft. Nineteen more were found against the locked doors, and twenty-five dead workers were crowded together in a cloakroom. When the police began taking the bodies away to the **morgue**, thousands of people followed them. At the morgue, they walked past the rows of bodies in an attempt to identify friends and family. This was a horrible experience for people, some of whom lost more than one immediate family member. Among the 146 victims, seven people were never identified.

Chapter Four

After the Fire

A flower-filled carriage leads the funeral procession for the Triangle fire victims through a crowd of thousands on April 5, 1911.

A Funeral March

A week after the Triangle fire, a funeral was held for the seven unnamed victims. On April 5, 1911, a cold rainy day, more than 120,000 people filled the streets of New York City in honor of the dead. Businesses in the area closed and the city grieved for several days.

Who Was to Blame?

The victims' families and friends were suffering, but they were also very angry. Newspapers began criticizing the factory's owners and the government for not preventing the Triangle fire, but no one wanted to take the blame.

Within the garment industry, Max Blanck and Isaac Harris, owners of the Triangle factory, were known as the "shirtwaist kings." Harris was in charge of running the factory—he would often walk up and down the aisles checking on workers. Blanck was in charge of marketing and selling the garments.

Max Blanck and Isaac Harris.

After the fire, Blanck and Harris were charged with **manslaughter**. Many of the witnesses at the trial testified that the doors in the factory had been locked. The jurors did not convict Blanck and Harris, however, because there was no absolute proof the owners knew the doors were locked.

The newspapers attacked Blanck and Harris, but the criticism did little to hurt their profits. They moved the Triangle factory out of the burnt Asch building to other premises and continued making money from shirtwaists.

The Building Department insisted it had performed its duty. The Fire Department explained that it did not have the power to make owners install safety features.

The owner of the building, Joseph Asch, and the owners of the Triangle factory said they were innocent, too. Blanck and Harris were never convicted of any crimes in connection with the Triangle fire.

Obeying the Law

"I have obeyed the law to the letter. There was not one detail of the construction of my building that was not submitted to the Building and Fire departments. Every detail was approved and the Fire Marshall congratulated me."

Joseph Asch, owner of the Asch building, March 25, 1911

Public Outrage

The public was outraged and began to call for change. People did not want the workers of the Triangle factory to have died in vain. If the law could not punish those responsible or prevent a similar fire, then the law needed to be changed.

The public outcry had an effect. The New York **legislature** created a Factory Investigating Commission to inspect and report on factories in the state of New York. The Commission was an important step forward for poor working people.

Too Much Blood

"This is not the first time girls have been burned alive in the city. Every week I must learn of the untimely death of one of my sister workers. Every year thousands of us are maimed. The life of men and women is so cheap and property is so sacred. . . . I know from my experience it is up to the working people to save themselves."

Rose Schneiderman, speaking at a meeting,
New York City, April 2, 1911

Newspaper cartoons showed that people would not forget the Triangle fire. The public demanded regulation of the workplace.

This Is One of a Hundred Murdered

Is any one to be punished for this?

24

Rose Schneiderman was born in Poland and moved at the age of six to the United States, where she was raised in orphanages. She became vice president of the New York WTUL in 1907. During the shirtwaist strike, Schneiderman picketed with the workers and was arrested. After the Triangle fire, she made a famous speech, saying that change should come through an uprising of the working class. Schneiderman was an inspector for the Factory Investigating Commission and became the national president of the WTUL in 1926. She was later an advisor on labor issues to President Franklin D. Roosevelt, and she continued to be a champion for working people until her death in 1972.

The Commission Gets to Work

The Commission's investigators spoke to hundreds of people, from factory owners and workers to firefighters and safety experts. Between 1911 and 1914, the state of New York passed thirty-six new laws, changing factory life in important ways. Companies now had to register their businesses and state how many people they employed. New laws limited the hours that women and children could work. At last, fire and safety regulations were introduced in factories.

Conclusion

Gaining Rights

Before the Triangle fire, workers in city factories had been powerless to demand change. Business owners would sacrifice the health and safety of their workers so they could make more money. The unions tried to improve the situation, but they could not fight big business on their own.

Labor Day

The first Labor Day, created to honor working people, was celebrated on September 5, 1882, in New York City. The event included a parade and a festival to entertain workers and their families. In 1884, the holiday was moved to the first Monday in September. On June 28, 1894, Congress passed an act making Labor Day an official holiday that continues to be celebrated every year in the United States.

The first Labor Day parade passes through Union Square in New York City in 1882.

After the fire, government was pulled into the battle—factories became **regulated** and workers gained many rights. The Triangle factory workers lost their lives, but workers in the future could demand safety in the workplace.

The Building

The building that held the Triangle factory still stands in New York City. It is now called the Brown building, and it is a national historic landmark because of its importance to the labor movement. The building is used by New York University for classrooms and offices. If it were to catch fire today, the students and workers inside would be able to escape. They would have the help of fire escapes, sprinklers, and fire drills, thanks to the reforms that took place after the Triangle fire.

Labor Today

Some business owners in the United States, however, operate **sweatshops** with horrible working conditions similar to those during the Industrial Revolution. Often, these sweatshops are garment shops that the government knows nothing about. The workers are often illegal immigrants with no unions to help them. They are usually paid far less than they need to survive, even though they work long hours at exhausting jobs. The struggle for better working conditions continues today.

A plaque on the Brown building commemorates the site where 146 workers died in the Triangle fire. In this picture, a garment worker stands in front of the plaque with a wreath placed there by UNITE, which is the name of the ILGWU today.

Time Line

1882	September 5: First Labor Day parade.
1886	American Federation of Labor (AFL) is founded.
1894	Congress declares Labor Day an official holiday.
1900	Several garment trades combine to create the International Ladies' Garment Workers' Union (ILGWU).
1901	January 15: Construction of Asch building is completed.
1903	The Women's Trade Union League (WTUL) is formed in New York City.
1906	Triangle Shirtwaist Company opens factory at the top of Asch building.
1909	Fire prevention expert recommends improvements in fire safety at Triangle factory, none of which is carried out.
	November: Shirtwaist workers in New York City go on strike.
1910	February 15: Shirtwaist strike ends.
	October 15: Asch building passes routine fire inspection.
	November 25: Fire kills twenty-five workers at a factory in Newark, New Jersey.
1911	March 25: Fire kills 146 people at the Triangle factory.
	April 5: Thousands of people attend funeral march for unnamed fire victims in New York City.
	April 11: Isaac Harris and Max Blanck are charged with manslaughter.
	June 30: New York State Factory Investigating Commission is created.
	December 5: Harris and Blanck trial begins.
	December 27: Harris and Blanck are found not guilty of manslaughter.

Things to Think About and Do

Working Children

Until the early twentieth century, American children from poor families usually worked. Find out what you can about child factory workers around the time of the Industrial Revolution. Imagine you are a child working in a factory in the early 1900s. Write about your working life. What is your job? How are you treated? What are some of your experiences?

The Role of Unions

As factories sprang up in American cities, workers formed unions to gain rights in the workplace. Imagine you are in charge of a union for workers in a particular field today—for example, you could choose to represent nurses, computer makers, or road construction workers. What demands would you make of employers to get good working conditions for your members? You should think about people's health, safety, and right to fair treatment. What else do you think is important for workers?

Fighting the Fire

Imagine you are a firefighter at the Triangle factory fire in 1911. Write an account of what you saw and what you did.

Glossary

garment: piece of clothing.

immigrant: person who comes to a new country to make his or her home.

industry: kind of business or work, especially work in factories involving manufacturing or other production on a large scale.

legislature: group of officials with the power to make laws.

manslaughter: crime of unintentionally causing the death of another person.

morgue: place where dead bodies are taken for examination or to be claimed by relatives.

picket: make a protest outside a place, such as a business where workers are striking for better conditions.

reform: change designed to improve conditions.

reformer: person who campaigns for or introduces reforms.

regulate: control employment or other practices with regulations or laws.

sanitary: clean enough not to be a health hazard.

scab: term used by strikers for a person who is hired in place of a striking worker; or who goes to work at his or her workplace in spite of a strike; or who crosses a picket line to do business when a strike is in progress.

strike: work stoppage in protest of working conditions or employers' actions.

suffragette: woman who fought for suffrage, which means the right to vote.

sweatshop: crowded factory with bad working conditions.

tenement: crowded apartment house, usually in a poor part of a city.

union: organization that campaigns and negotiates for better working conditions for its members, who are usually workers from a particular trade or kind of business.

unsanitary: so dirty as to be unhealthy.

ventilation: access to fresh air.

Further Information

Books

Bartoletti, Susan Campbell. *Kids on Strike!* Houghton Mifflin, 1999.

Littlefield, Holly. *Fire at the Triangle Factory*. Carolrhoda, 1996.

McCormick, Anita Louise. *The Industrial Revolution* (In American History). Enslow, 1998.

Stein, R. Conrad. *The Pullman Strike and the Labor Movement* (In American History). Enslow, 2001.

Woog, Adam. *A Sweatshop During the Industrial Revolution* (Working Life). Lucent, 2002.

Web Sites

www.ilr.cornell.edu/trianglefire/ The School of Industrial and Labor Relations at Cornell University has an excellent online exhibition about the Triangle fire.

www.uniteunion.org/kids/kids.html Children's web page provided by UNITE, the present-day garment workers' union that replaced the ILGWU. Has information about sweatshops and a story that explores the topic of child labor.

www.uniteunion.org/research/history/historyinaction.html Another web page provided by UNITE, with information about women who led the reform movement in the garment industry.

Useful Addresses

American Labor Museum
Botto House National Landmark
83 Norwood Street
Haledon, NJ 07508
Telephone: (973) 595-7953

Index